# Meg's book

Illustrated by Nina O'Connell

**Meg's eggs**  page 2

**The log**  page 6

**The big seed**  page 11

Nelson

# Meg's eggs

"I have one egg.
Look at my egg,"
said Meg.

"I have two eggs.
Look at my eggs,"
said Meg.

"I have three eggs.
Look at my eggs,"
said Meg.

"Come and see my eggs.
Come and look."

# The log

One chick got on the log.

Two chicks got on the log.

Three chicks got on the log.

Pat the pig got on the log.
"No, no, no,"
said the chicks.

# The big seed

"Here is a seed," said Meg.

"It is very big.

I will plant it."

So she did.

"I will get some water,"
said Meg.
So she did.

"Look at it now," said Meg.
"I will get some
more water."
So she did.

The seed grew and grew.

It grew as big as the chicks.

It grew as big as Meg.

"The seed looks like the sun," said Meg.
"It is a sunflower."

"We can eat all the seeds," said Meg.
And they did.